PONDERING THOUGHTS

Lorna Ramirez

Published in Australia by Lorna Ramirez
First published in Australia February 2018
This edition published 2019
Copyright © Lorna Ramirez 2019
Cover design, typesetting: WorkingType Studio

The right of Lorna Ramirez to be identified as the Author of the Work has been asserted in accordance with the Copyright, Designs and Patents Act 1988.

All rights reserved. No part of this publication may be reproduced, stored in a retrieval system, or transmitted, in any form or by any means without the prior written permission of the publisher, nor be otherwise circulated in any form of binding or cover other than that in which it is published and without a similar condition being imposed on the subsequent purchaser.

Ramirez, Lorna
Pondering Thoughts
PBK: 978-0-6482130-6-2
EBOOK: 978-0-6482130-7-9
pp114

About the Author

Lorna Ramirez was born, raised and educated in Manila in the Philippines, attaining a degree in chemical engineering and working as a laboratory manager in a textiles company.

In 1977, with her husband and her son and daughter, she migrated to Australia. She worked as a laboratory technician and a chemist in Australia, only retiring in the year 2000 to care for her first grandchild.

Lorna Ramirez has travelled extensively, gaining much from her interactions with people all over the world and building a strong foundation for her philosophies about life. She loves gardening, cooking and reading and playing the piano. She is also interested in the stock exchange.

She has published five books: *My Innermost Thoughts* 2014, *My Passion My Calling* 2015, *Moments of Love, Lust and Ecstasy* 2017, *Reflective Contemplations* 2018 and the latest is *Pondering Thoughts* 2019. She won third prize for the 2017 Christmas Writing Competition by the Society of Women Writers of Victoria. In October 2016 Lorna was one of the recipients of a certificate of recognition from FILCCA (Filipino Community Council of Australia).

Lorna is also a regular contributor for *The Philippine Times* in Melbourne and *The Philippine Sentinel* in Sydney. Throughout her life Lorna Ramirez, a woman of faith, has been a wise observer of human behaviour and has collected her many wisdoms and observations to produce this inspiring and uplifting book.

Acknowledgements

Special Thanks to Alyssa Cary
my Personal Assistant

Dedicated To

My loving husband, Claro
Grandchildren Alyssa and Amelia
Children and their partners:
Carlo and Marie
Maria and Steve
My sister Victoria Polon

1
Of Human and Divine Love

"Loving someone does not mean you love "GOD" less" A meaningful and touching phrase explained by the Mother Superior to Maria from the movie *The Sound of Music*. Indeed, it is true that many are called but few are chosen. Love is like a thief in the night, it can strike anyone without warning

I am truly blessed to experience both divine and human love. In my late teens I felt the blissful happiness of divine love. In that moment, praying was another realm of my spiritual soul which transformed me to find a joyful connection with "God". I found complete serenity and tranquillity with him. Praying in the church gave me an unexplained exultation that enveloped my body and soul.

Every Sunday I would spend the whole day at the church doing church activities, and having religious meetings. It is at this point that my parents began to get worried that I might follow the footsteps of my cousins who entered the monastery.

Then someone had touched my innocent and fragile heart, I cried, prayed and asked why me? He was a young seminarian who was soon to be an ordained priest . No words were spoken between us, but our body language, smiles and the expressions of our eyes said it all. I was confused and felt a different kind of love.

Of course I attended his ordination, and shook his hands to

congratulate him after the ceremony. He squeezed my hands tightly and with a tender tone in his voice he said" I am sorry". I replied in a small voice as I looked down unable to meet his gaze I said" I understand"

Moving on I concentrated on my studies and finished my B.S in Chemical Engineering, then, was lucky to get a job as an industrial chemist in a textile industry where I met my husband.

Out of the blue one Sunday evening at a restaurant, I bumped in to the priest. I broke the news to him that I would be getting married in the next few months. He graciously offered his service to be the officiating priest. And I gladly accepted .

At the wedding reception he asked me , if I was happy with the love that I had found. I quickly responded and with a smile on my face" I said "I am very happy." That was the last time I saw him.

I have no regrets with my life now. I have husband who is very supportive in all my passions and even cares to all my whims and caprices. A husband who loves me so dearly. , with whom I raised two successful children and have two wonderful grandchildren. I could not ask for more

I firmly believe, whatever love you choose, be it love to family,, priests, missionaries , soldiers , country or God they are all the same, they take and give us dedication, commitment and responsibility.

An excerpt from my book,
Innermost Thoughts

At times we cry within
Yet no one can hear
The pain and heart, only you can feel
Those shattered dreams and memories of yesteryears
That haunt you vividly as only they can
But That was then and today is different
Years have passed and things have changed
Once again, Triumphantly you emerge now
A better stronger person

2
Perfect Imperfection

TO BE PERFECT IS TO BE IMPERFECT. What is imperfection? It is a fault, flaw, a disfigurement distorted, and the descriptive lists go on and on. Imperfection will always be abhorred by many. A lot of us will aim and desire for perfection in everything we do. However there are lessons to be learned for being imperfect. We can as well learned from the mistakes of others, and make these work for your own advantage.

Imperfections inspire us to be creative, to be strong, and compassionate. A pianist will endure hours of practice each day to overcome his imperfection and to achieve perfection in playing classical pieces with ease and confidence. A rough diamond will be turned into an exquisite expensive stone desired by many., thanks to the creative skilled hands of a diamond cutter. An aspiring chef, will diligently work to perfect their own signature dish. These are only a few examples how imperfection can lead to perfection.

Imperfection challenges us to work harder to reach your ultimate goal and be the best of what you are. Imperfection makes us compassionate and fully understand the feelings and suffering of other people especially who share the same problems you are going through.

Nonetheless there are also an ugly side of being a perfectionist.

Being a perfectionist will lead to stress, mental blackout, and at times depression. Being a perfectionist you doubt other people abilities, thus unable to delegate the work and the end result will be discontentment., unhappiness and exhaustion.

How can we deal with imperfections?..... There are several ways to deal with Imperfections, first and foremost we should remember that no one is perfect. We all have our own shortcomings and flaws.

Secondly just enjoy life itself, and if you have physical disabilities, try to overcome them by adjusting what is comfortable with your situations. There are those people with no legs and arms but still live normal life by conquering their own challenges and becoming more than they could imagine. Know your limitations and explore your talents especially for those with physical disabilities. They can be good in sport, writing, and music.

Do not compare yourself with others, as It can lead to disappointments, and frustrations. Each of us is different and special in our own way. Imagine if we lived in a perfect world with perfect people around, life will be boring and uninteresting. Always count your blessings and this will put a smile on your face.

I believe that once you reach your goal of being nearly perfect in life whether it be a success in career, financial status, fame family, we must always remain humble as we can or else perfection is irrelevant.

Excerpt from
Reflective Contemplations

I believe that life does not need to be perfect
Imperfection Challenges, motivates, stimulates
The desire to grow and be a better person
Imperfection makes us humble
Helps us to accept, things we can not change
Imperfection enables us to see life
From a different perspective
Perhaps so, we can see more in depth meaning
Of what life is all about

3
Pondering Thoughts

Heard melodies are sweet but those unheard are sweeter, an excerpt from Ode On A Grecian Urn written by the romantic poet John Keats. This is one of my favourite poems. There are so many interpretations of this verse and my own is of someone you are so much in love with and words are not enough to express your feelings, but when manifested with actions such as the sacrifices you are willing to do for your loved ones, it will be more potent than all the descriptive words spoken.

The first week of September is the celebration of Father's Day and I dedicate this article for all the fathers in the world. Most fathers are subdued in expressing their emotions, however they will always do whatever it takes to protect their families from all unexpected events and predicaments They appear to be strong and a disciplinarian. In actuality, deep within they have a soft spot for their children especially their daughters. Arguably Fathers are the foundation of a family unit but of course with the help of mothers. Fathers have a major role in the development of their children. Children who have a wholesome relationship with their fathers, grow up to be a well balances and happy responsible adults.

In today's environment, fathers have a myriad role in the family. They are not only seen as a bread winner but also take an active part in household chores and the upbringing of their children. Every Father's Day, I always remember my Dad. Like the verse in the Ode On A Grecian Urn, my father is a man of few words. Yet his heart was as big as the universe and beyond. He had helped his brothers and sisters as well as my mom's brothers and sisters to be able to finish their university degrees in Manila. He was a person who will give his last money in his pocket to anyone asking for help.

I still remember his smile, that was warm as the morning sun, his laughter was so infectious like the sound of the echo of the roaring seas. His eyes will sparkle like the stars in the sky of happiness every time he was surrounded with loved ones, families and friends. His generosity, kindness and joyous nature continue to resonate with me, thus having an impact and tremendous influence in all my writings. I love and miss you DAD……. Really I Do

Excerpt from
Reflective Contemplations

It is not enough to say the word
"I LOVE YOU"
To your loved ones
It Must be manifested by actions
Or else the words will be meaningless

4
Winter Season in Our Lives

There will always be a Winter Season in our lives regardless who you are, and no one can be spared.

Just like cold and dreary season of winter, there are times in our lives that winter falls upon us through the loss of loved ones, loss of a friend, health issues, job loss or the end of a relationship. It will be the lowest ebb in our lives.

For some it can be manageable, they can survive the season and they can re-assess, reflect and move on. Sadly others just can not cope, that which will be detrimental for their health and can at times result to family breakdown

My friend from overseas couldn't cope or come to terms with the loss of their first born child. Depression, and failing health slowly overtaking her body and soul. Supports from families and friends seemed futile and she saw no reason to live ., because of the unfortunate situation, her husband left her, and that only added to her misery. And resulted in her ending her own life.

I truly believe that "GOD" should be our refuge in times of our troubles and heartaches. At times your strong faith in "HIM" through prayers will help and guide you and through this you can find your inner strength to overcome all the obstacles in life.

A gardener will always plan, prepare, and improve his garden in preparation for the coming Spring Season. It is the time for a gardener to plant new beautiful bulbs, bare rooted roses for an exquisite display of colourful flowers in Spring and Summer Seasons. Trees, fruit trees with no leaves an eye sore to us will be transformed into arrays and display of different magnificent dazzling colours in Spring and Summer.

Akin to a gardener, Winter season in our lives will be the time for contemplation, meditation, planning, learning the lessons from our mistakes, failures and an eye opener.. It can be a guiding light for a better future, because after all, Spring will follow and this will be the beginning of a new life, new hope for a brighter tomorrow. We need winter season in our lives to truly appreciate more the joy of having Spring and Summer seasons in our lives.

Excerpt from
Reflective Contemplations

SEASONS OF LIFE
In every stage in life we had
In every journey and experience we had
For every hardship, sorrow and pain
There will always be an end
Just like Winter cold and woeful
Spring will always follow
Alive and blissful
Forgetting the dark miserable Winter night
And moving to a bright new life
For a fresh beginning and a new way of life

Pondering Thoughts | Lorna Ramirez

5
The Wheel Of Life

Goodbye for the past year and welcome to the coming year.. Another year has gone and we are a year older and wiser. This is a time for soul searching, reflection, and reassessment of things to do to make the coming year better, rosier and more successful than the year before.

It seems only yesterday that my family celebrated our very first New Year in Australia. That was forty years ago, and in those days 'celebrations of Christmas and New year were very subdued; a far cry from todays environment or compared to what it is today,

As migrant in the late 70's we worked hard, hence we were able to buy our first home. As the children were growing up and the prospect of my parents in laws coming to Australia to live with us, we moved to a bigger house in a nearby suburb. It was a quiet courtyard. Our neighbours were mostly pensioners and retirees. We were one of the youngest families in the area. In those days we bonded with our neighbours and at times participated in street celebrations for Christmas and New Year.

As time passed by, most of them had gone to the nursing home or passed away. Now we have became the oldest family in the neighbourhood, witnessing a complete change of age demographic in our area.

Our children had moved out and started their own families. Our house that was once full of activities, laughter and chaos is peaceful and quiet now. Indeed, a wheel of life. Back to basic just the two of us once again.

How long do we able to maintain our big house? How long can my husband be able to care for our back garden? Scary thoughts, but for now we just move on. We are so lucky that we are still healthy and enjoying the love and company of family and friends.

For how long will my husband and I will be able to celebrate together Christmas and New Year?.....My wish is to hopefully celebrate for another twenty more years or so!

Excerpt from
Reflective Contemplations

ETERNAL FLAME

One of the sweetest things in life
Is to be able to share moments
With your loved ones up to the
Last journey of your life
To be able to look back together
Those beautiful and unforgettable memories
To be able to grow old together
Learning to accept each others
Faults and shortcomings
To be able to let the flame of love
We always cherish be
Forever in our hearts
Will remain as passionate as ever

5 The Wheel Of Life

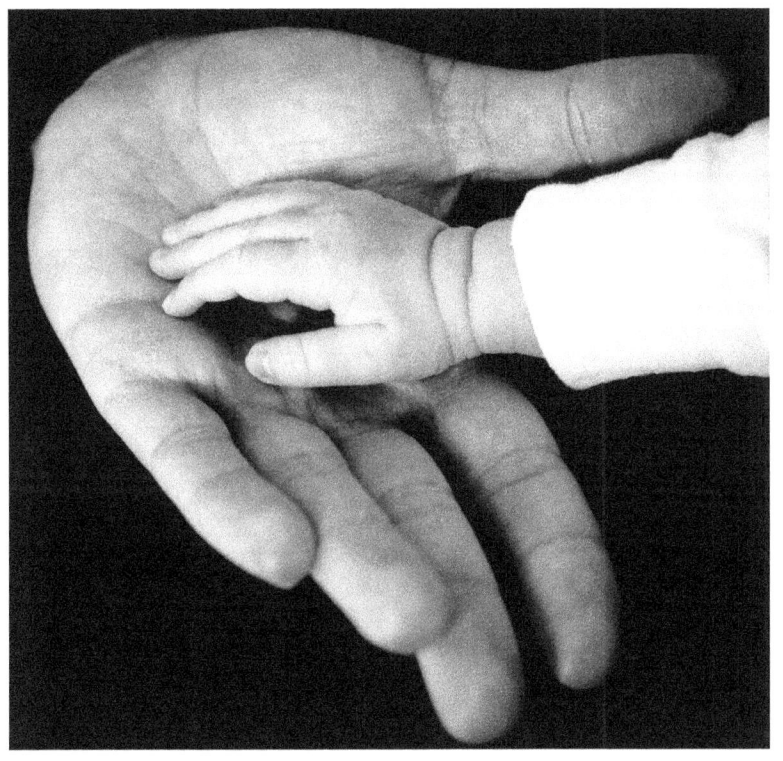

6
A Christmas Story
(True Story)

The Christmas season will always bring joy and happiness to all of us, and in the Philippines, it is one of the most celebrated events of the year. The Christmas of 1963 was the most memorable Christmas I'd ever had, and here is my story

In my younger days in the Philippines I was very active in our church and was the President of the Legion Of Mary at the Christ the King Church, Project 7 in Quezon city. This consisted of activities and duties such as catechism and leading block rosaries to name a few. One of the apostolic works that we did was visiting parishioners during weekends to spread the word of God and to support the elderly of our community.

While doing my apostolic work, I befriended an elderly lady by the name of Lola Rose. She was in her mid-eighties, with no family apart from her only son who was living in America with his wife and two sons. After Sunday's morning mass and church meeting, I always visited her. She would bake my favourite Chiffon and Cassava cakes.. We shared the same interests: in reading inspirational books and playing classical piano pieces. We talked about a lot of things , and every time she talked about her son and grandchildren , she would show a twinkle in her eyes.

Every December Lola Rose's son and his family come and visit her, and every Christmas eve I would visit her .and experience a great feeling of warmth to be a part of this beautiful family. On Christmas Eve she always cooked Pancit (noodle), Leche Plan (crème Caramel) Puto (rice cake) and Dinuguan (pork blood stew) and of course a little gift wrapped with a beautiful ribbon as present for me.

One Sunday morning when I visited her she was crying, she said that her son won't be able to visit her this Christmas . Embracing her I assured her that she won't be lonely as my family will be there for her.

As promised I told my Dad on Christmas eve that I will be going early to visit Lola Rose , and then would head to the church afterwards in time for Christmas Eve Mass.. The door was open when I arrived at her house, but when I called her name there was no answer. I thought she must be asleep, so I let myself in. Passing through the kitchen I noticed she had already prepared the Leche Plan, Pancit puto and dinguan and a nice wrapped gift for me. Smiling I went to the bedroom, there was a note at the bedside saying " Dear Lorna, I am so tired I will have a small nap, please wake me up once you have arrived.

Lola was sleeping peacefully with a rosary on her hand, As I began to tenderly wake her up ,she was not responding to my voice and as I touched her, the body was cold as ice. I screamed and started sobbing in a confused panic ,my whole body ,trembling with shock

It will be more than five decades now since that harrowing experience but I will always remember with love the good old memories I shared with this lovely lady whom I fondly called as my Lola Rose.

Excerpt from
My Innermost Thoughts

Death will always leave
A gaping hole in our hearts
It will take time to heal
But, all the beautiful memories
Will always be Treasured

7
Life Begins at "Any Age"

Contrary to a popular adage " Life Begins At Forty" I truly believe that Life Begins At Any Age. It was in the year 1932 that, an American Psychologist and writer Walter Pitkin, published a self help book which started the notion that Life begins at forty, hence pioneering the saying.

Every person is different . Depending upon the person's situational circumstance or even luck can play an important and major role in the lives of all of us. "Life Begins at Forty "is no longer relevant in today's environment. People live longer and are able to achieve and maximise their talents up to the twilight years of their lives.

There are people who are very successful at a very young age. Mark Zuckerberg launched his Face Book from his dormitory at the age of 20 on February 4, 2004 making him a billionaire at a very young age. Other examples include singers and artists, one of them is Justin Bieber at the age of 16 became a household name and rose to stardom,

Sometimes success and fame overtake their young minds and souls, and they succumb to drugs and alcohols culminating to the end of their lives. Amy Winehouse, River Phoenix and many more talented artists, singers , are some whose lives were cut short because of the pressure of fame. However there are late bloomers, who discover and pursue their talents from their 70's and through their 90's.

At the age of 95, Nola Ochs from Jetmore Kansas graduated from the University in 2007 She was certified by the Guinness World Records as the oldest person to have a University degree. Grandma Moses, without basic training, started painting at the age of 75. And at the age of 101, one of her paintings was sold for $1.2 million dollars.

I started writing at age of 69, a talent that I did not know I had. Now I have published four books and a regular contributor of articles to the Philippine Times. Two years ago I decided to continue and pursue my passion for playing classical pieces, I enrolled in a Music School and next year I will be doing AMEB exam (Australian Music Examination Board) for grade eight intermediate level. This is prime time of my life definitely a late bloomer.

We should never stop learning, never stop doing exciting things and sometimes doing things out of our comfort zone, it is the spice of life We should continue to socialise and be active. Continue to be motivated and you will be surprised of what you can achieve. Suffice to say, the popular saying of Life begins at 40 is definitely obsolete in this modern technological era of TODAY!

Excerpt from
My Innermost Thoughts

Never stop learning
Never stop stimulating your brain
Never stop believing in yourself
Never stop following your dreams
Never stop doing things
You are passionate about
Continually Challenge yourself
After all life is too short
To be wasting your precious time.

8
Spring of Life

Spring is my favourite season of the year Why? Because I believe Spring is full of surprises, excitements and adventures. It is a refreshing and enjoyable season to experience. The days become longer and the temperature becomes more pleasant.

My hither and thither plants and shrubs from the last Winter season are looking tidier since my husband started to spend more time in the garden. My roses Geranium and annuals are now in bloom, showcasing their magnificent flowers in rainbow colours, a feast for the eyes. A remarkable beauty of nature is to be experienced in Spring.

My Cherry, apple, Apricot, Plum, and Peach are all blossoming at their peak indicative of the abundance of fruits this coming Summer season. The fragrance smell of Jasmin flowers filled up my backyard garden especially during the night.

While doing my morning walk I can hear and see the birds coming back to the garden. Bees and butterflies are busy doing their jobs, sucking nectar from flower to flower. Spring is also the busiest season for the Honey- Bee and the Beekeeper

One of the many surprises of Spring are the deciduous plants , trees, shrubs which hibernate during Winter, and are now showing sign of life and growing stronger each day.

Why do we truly appreciate and welcome the Spring season? Because it is a stark contrast of the gloomy, dreary cold Winter season. Akin to our life's journey, the more adversities and struggles in life that we go through The more we appreciate the real essence of what happiness is all about. The more we can savour and value the joy of the sweet success in life.

Spring denotes life, hope and new beginning. So what are we waiting for? Spring into action and start doing things you put on hold. This is the time to pursue our goals and aspirations in life. Lets enjoy the Spring season as much as we can while it is here!

Excerpt from
My Innermost Thoughts

The season of Winter is akin to the darkest moments
Of our lives
Unforeseen traumatic tragedies will happen
As long as you have a solid faith in God
And the support of loved ones and friends
You can overcome all predicaments
Soon Spring will be around
New hope, new life and new beginning
Our journey will be rosier
And joyful than ever

9
Worlds Apart

We all have our own journeys to the countries and destinations of our choosing. Whether it will be for business, holiday or balikbayan (overseas Filipino tourists), they will have memorable experiences and exciting adventures . My recent travel to Manila early this year was an unforgettable one that I would like to share to all.

With no immediate families such as parents and siblings in Manila, we stayed at a five star hotel in Makati. The hotel was a walking distance to SM, Glorietta, Greenbelt and Landmark(these are all shopping malls) As we entered the hotel I was overwhelmed by the luxury of the place. With Humongous foyer with magnificent chandelier, and the two grand stairways leading to spacious second floor foyer, It was such a lavish display of luxury. On the end of the first floor foyer, was a huge open space café lounge where a 14 piece band will entertain, playing contemporary, classical, jazz and modern music.

The following day my cousin picked us up in their car to go to SSS (Social Security System) Cavite to help me to get my SSS pension It took us only less than an hour for the approval of my pension, however we have to find a bank for my remittance , then the fun started. Leaving our car at the SSS , we walked along a footpath crowded with makeshift stores, full of half naked men staring at us. I felt uncomfortable with the situations. It was so hot, sunny and I was the only one wearing sunglasses. Hubby whisper and said do not wear your sun glasses . On the way to the bank we had to hop into a moving jeepney vehicle. Lucky my husband was there to help me in, as I I had forgotten to jump on. Finally we found a bank to deposit my SSS pension

Then again I had another traumatic experience when crossing the street. Being at the outskirt of Manila there were no traffic lights, you have to cross at your own risk. Although there were white lines on the road for crossing, cars and buses won't give way to pedestrians. I screamed and nearly died crossing the street, but I managed to pull through.

There was a very sharp contrast from some wealthy areas and tourist belt in the city. You can see so much poverty, but the people were happy, still smiling and friendly. Happiness is really subjective there are those people who got everything but have no peace within. Material things had overtaken their souls and spirit. This contrast was brought further to light when we returned to the hotel, where we were greeted by smiling gorgeous ladies who were eager to give you everything your heart desires but at a cost

I do love to visit the Philippines, its raw, vibrant, energetic and the people were so friendly. They were willing always to help you. Amidst the misery and poverty around, they were still smiling contented in their lives. People connect and bonded with one another. Even at night you can see people in groups outside their houses having fun sharing stories and laughing. In Australia you do not even know your neighbour's name. Is it because we are too busy in Australia working , or busy to gain earthly and worldly things that you do not have time to connect with people?

Will I be going back again? Of course I will . I love the food, the people and still love the Filipino values and culture.

Returning back in Australia I do appreciate more all the blessings we do enjoy here. Most of the times we had taken it for granted We are truly lucky to be in this beautiful adopted country of ours... AUSTRALIA

My unpublished inspirational message

No matter what you do
No matter where you are
No matter what you are now
Whether you are successful or not
Do not forget your root
Where you came from

10
Is it Fate or Destiny?

Did you ever question yourself for a phenomenon or a significant event that happened in your life? Did you wonder if it is fate or destiny?

Hitherto, these two words, fate and destiny are often misunderstood by a lot of people. The truth is they are entirely different in concept. Fate is something that can not be altered, no matter how hard we try. It is a pre-determined event that can happen without our choice and is beyond our control. Destiny is something that we have full control of, a choice and the desire to make it happen. Nonetheless, there are times that fate and destiny can go hand in hand. and can work effectively together.

You can not choose your parents, relatives nor the country of your birth. You can not choose also the timing of your death. These are only few of the many examples of fate. With destiny you can have a choice, explore your given talents, and chase your dreams and most of all a choice to be successful in life.

In a religious point of view, Christians believe that GOD has an intention and mission for us here on earth, but He also has given us free will to do the righteous way of living. IF we chose the wrong path, we should be responsible for our actions.

James 4:2 (NIV) " You desire but do not have, so you kill, you covet but you can not get, so you quarrel and fight. You do not have, but you do not ask God"

Indeed this is an ultimate example of our free will, and the choices we made will have a dire consequences in our lives. We also have a choice of connecting with God, but some continuously ignore that, and some have taken it for granted.

This is one of the many series of experiences of fate and destiny in my life. Most of you will remember the Port Arthur Massacre in Tasmania on the 28th of April 1996. My hubby and I had booked to visit on that very same date, but ..I had changed the date to one week before to 21st of April as I was informed that there would be festivities of Military parade, Police concert and lots of activities that will be happening. The Port Arthur massacre happened on the 28 of April 1996 Sunday at 1:00 at the Broad Arrow Café. The day and time that we were supposed to have our lunch as part of our tour itinerary. The Broad Arrow Café was quite small and the arrangement of tables were so closed together that it was easy for Martin Bryant to shoot people at the café.

I always have a shiver down my spine every time I remember this incident. It was my fate not to die yet, I believe I still have to fulfil a mission here on earth. At times there are occurrences that will happen in our lives that only God will know and have control of. Yes it is true we have a free will, a destiny to chase and follow but at the end it is the will of God that will prevail. The Lord's prayer venerated and prayed by billions of Christians around the world has this important message

"THY WILL BE DONE ON EARTH AS IT IS IN HEAVEN:

Excerpt from
My Innermost Thoughts

Realities of Life

Each time we breathe to live

Each time we should remember that life is a gamble

Each time is a challenge

Each time is a journey because no one knows

What the future brings and holds

Yes we can try to plan and control our lives

But much to our dismay we soon discover

We can only do it to a certain degree

So as not to be bitterly disappointed, accept the things

You can not change

If you can change things, do them better next time

Indeed these are the REALITIES OF LIFE

11
For the Love of God

FATHER FORGIVE THEM, FOR THEY KNOW NOT WHAT THEY ARE DOING. Luke 23:34. Today you will be with me in paradise, Luke 23:43. These were the first and second last words of Christ on the cross. Christ humbled himself accepting the will of God to die for our sins. These are the real substance of the meaning of Lent, that is to practice humility and forgiveness as manifested by our lord Jesus Christ.

Lent is the most important celebration and commemoration of the death of Christ on the cross by all Christians around the world. Lent is the 40 days celebrations before Easter (the time of the resurrection of Christ) This is the time for reflections, fasting, repentance, spiritual discipline and most of all forgiveness and humility. After Lenten season, there will be Easter family celebrations, Easter egg hunting, lots of chocolates and sweets. Joyous celebrations for Christ resurrection. For non -believers this is a time for holidays and time off from work. Nonetheless for Christians , no matter how earnest and intense your prayers are, if your heart is full of hate, greed or envy, the sacred time is meaningless.

During the Lenten season countries from different congregation will have their own ways of celebrating. Generally, they make small sacrifices such as giving up certain things they enjoy doing. Some people fast and abstain from eating meat during Lenten Fridays. In the Philippines even though the Catholic church disapproves of performing the penitence , there are people whipping themselves on their backs with bundles of bamboo sticks tied to a length of rope . until their backs will be covered with blood. People are still doing this for repentance of sins.

The Lenten season is also a reminder to all of us that amidst all the suffering and conflict we are going through, there will always be a glimmer of hope, akin to the celebration of Easter, the resurrection of Christ.

According to Matthew 7:23 Christ said " Not everyone who said LORD, LORD will enter the kingdom of heaven, but the one who does the will of my Father WHO is in heaven. "In the realm of religion and Christianity we are encourage to go to church every Sunday to pray and give homage to GOD. However, there are those who pray often and regularly , yet their hearts are as cold as ice and full of deceit . Will they have a place in Heaven? In contrast There are agnostic, atheist people but their hearts are pure, kind and caring, Will these people have a place in heaven. Indeed these are two extreme examples, but I firmly believe that your actions, the way you treat people , and if you have an inner peace within yourself and others , is what really matter

Excerpt from
My Innermost Thoughts

Prayers are not the only way to communicate with God
There are other ways, such as a simple act of kindness to others
I am close to mother nature while working in my garden
I can show my appreciation of all the beautiful creations
He had given us
I am a good mother, grandmother, friend and respect for others
Following all HIS commandments and what matters
most is following
All that HE preaches. These are more potent ways
Of expressing my love for "HIM" other than prayers!!

12
The Most Beautiful Face on Earth

A little boy was crying, looking for his mother. A stranger came and ask the little boy, "where is your mum and can you describe what does she look like?" which the little boy replied" My mum has the most beautiful face on earth" The stranger, in search for a beautiful lady and said to the boy, " Is this your mum ?" the boy said ' No my mum is prettier than her. A few times the stranger tried to bring beautiful ladies and each time the boy said that his mum is prettier. Then a plain looking lady came and said " There you are I had been looking for you !" The little boy's face brightened with gladness and proudly said to the stranger, " You see my mum has the most beautiful face on earth"

Indeed, through the eyes of children their mothers are the most beautiful for them, true to the saying that BEAUTY IS IN THE EYES OF THE BEHOLDER.

A face that only a mother can love is another expression we say about the unconditional love a mother can offer to her children. From the moment of conception, followed by birth and the first taste of milk of a baby from their mother's bosom, There is an immeasurable bonding between a mother and her child.

While the children are growing up they will feel and vision their mothers as a protector, who gives them love and kindness and showers them with lots of hugs and kisses . Thus in their minds without any doubt their mother will be the most wonderful and beautiful person on earth..

Those sleepless nights, sacrifices made especially for working mums, a mother will endure to nurture and care for their children. A mother is a teacher, disciplinarian, provider, protector, mediator rolled in to one. No job can outdo what mother can do and I believe being a mother is the most noble, challenging, and difficult job, but its all worth it !!!.

Mothers have a big influence in shaping the character of their children. A responsible mother will produce responsible adults because mothers serve as a role model for their children. This is a precious gift all mothers can offer to the society and the wider community.

It is fleeting to say just for that special day of every 2nd Sunday of May, we should all toast to celebrate and ,recognise the significant role of all mothers in the world. However our appreciation for them should always be given at all times..............

HAPPY MOTHER'S
DAY TO ALL THE BEAUTIFUL MOTHERS
AROUND THE WORLD!!

Excerpt from
My Passion My Calling

MOTHERS

It is in the mother's heart

That children can find

Assurance of being loved

It is in the mother's arms

That the children can find

Solace and comfort

BUT

It is in the mother's hugs and kisses

That the children can find the real joy

Pondering Thoughts | Lorna Ramirez

13
Thanks for the Memories

Each year will come and go, so will be this year. At the end of each year we are always in the process of preparing, assessing and evaluating the things we had done and had happened in our lives. There are memories that can be forgotten but there are some that can linger on forever and will always makes us happy.

Both pleasant and painful memories can happen for the past year, and for the unfortunate ones, this is the time to move on and try to embrace the coming new year with hope, new life and a new beginning. From the past mistakes we can now set up new goals and aspirations. For grieving families who lost loved ones, remember to concentrate for the living loved ones who still need your care and support.

It is no use having a long list of New Year's resolution. Based from statistic only 8% people will keep their New Year's resolution. Nonetheless remember that the choices we made will create and shape our future.

Be practical and sensible when making a resolution, start with the easiest one, take baby step and when you feel you are ready you can set or aim for your next goal. By doing this it won't create disappointment and frustrations.

Prioritise what is important, but consider as well that your changes will benefit not only yourself but your loved ones. Ask you family for support if needed and I am sure they will always be there for you.

I am truly thankful for the memories for the year 2017. It was the year that we celebrated our 50th wedding anniversary, the same year I had launched my 3rd book and my first novel "Moments of Love, Lust and Ecstasy. The previous year I decided to continue my piano study and fortunate enough to pass the Australian Music Examination Board for intermediate level (AMEB).

This time I won't be making any New Year's Resolution instead I will continue my passion for writing, music and supporting my Charities, most especially The National Breast Cancer Foundation.

Thanks for the outgoing year 2017 for all the wonderful memories I have and I hope next year ahead in 2018 will be the same or even better for me and for all of us.

Excerpt from
My Innermost Thoughts

Excerpt from my book
It is the choice we make in our lives
That makes life itself
Full of challenges and surprises
Hence shaping and creating
Our journey of life

14
The Many Faces of Happiness

Happy are those who can forgive
Because they will find peace
Within themselves and others
Happy are those who stay connected with God
Because it is the only way to eternal salvation
Happy are those who are willing to share and help others
Because they make a difference in this troubled world we live in
And lastly happy are those who can love and accept people
Because they will be loved in return

By Lorna Ramirez

Happiness will truly define who, what we are and what our priorities are in life. We go through different stages of happiness as we walk the journey of life. A small child will find happiness by playing with pots and pans or even by pulling tissues from a tissue box, ignoring expensive toys given by dotting parents. Expression of delight and joy on children's' faces when surrounded with candies, chocolates, cakes, and ice cream; those are simple gestures of happiness through the eyes of children.

As we grow older happiness becomes complicated. We set goals, achievements, and power. An ultimate happiness by many of us. For some people, there are those whose happiness can be achieved by sharing and helping others such as missionaries, community workers, soldiers, to name a few. They are special people who have talents that an "Almighty God" has provided them to share.

At the middle of our journey in life a different level of happiness is felt when we meet our soulmate or the love of our life, then becoming a parent. Sheer joy of happiness is experienced when we had our first born child. Our children are an extended version of ourselves, nurture them with love and they will do the same once they have families of their own. No greater happiness can be felt by parents knowing that their children lead a happy and successful life.

My own experience of happiness was that moment where I had the chance to hold my first born granddaughter. From the very first time that I laid eyes on her, I knew that I was blessed to be her grandmother. As I walk through life nearing the end of my journey, my happiness consists of looking after my grandchildren, being there for their first smile, first uttered words, and their first steps. It is an exuberant experience to be a grandmother, and I believe that all grandparents can relate to this.

As a guest speaker at one of the events that I attended I could feel the frustration and loneliness of the elderly. They felt left out and seeking for the attention, love, and care of their families. Fortunately in Australia, we have elderly organisations that are doing a fantastic job to help and entertain them with various activities that can alleviate their loneliness.

At the end we must remember that we will all grow old, and

when the time comes it's up to us to make our own lives interesting regardless of your age.

Akin to the happiness of a child, as we walk through the final journey our happiness becomes simple and uncomplicated. Indeed this is the cycle of life. As we grow older we also realise that *the simplest things in life are often the best.*

15
What's in a Smile?

A beautiful smile can melt anyone's heart, but what is really in a smile that inspires a poet to write, a musician to write songs about it, and Leonardo da Vinci to paint the Mona Lisa; the lady with a mysterious smile that captivates and fascinates all of us? Indeed do not underestimate the power of a smile.

How often do we meet and encounter strangers on the streets, shopping malls and indifferent places? Just a swift fleeting glance from them followed by a smile can mean a lot of things such as greetings; hello, how are you, wishing you the best of the day. A gesture that is more potent and powerful way of communicating other than words. The moment when you see loved ones, friends and relations, before uttering a word a smile from their faces says it all.

A smile is a symbol and image of our emotions and an expression of our inner self but nonetheless not all smiles are genuine and sincere. There are smiles that are deceiving, hurtful and insulting which is an ugly side of the human nature. There are those people who however, smile while hiding their frustration, sorrow and grief. They are the courageous ones who remain positive and continue to move on.

15 What's in a Smile?

We always smile in front of the camera because we want to be remembered as happy contented people who enjoy that very moment when the photo is taken. Who can forget that beautiful smile from your first crush, your first love? A thrilling and exhilarating special moment that we had. Likewise, those gorgeous smiles from your children and your grandchildren will always be cherished in your heart.

When your children and grandchildren were small and were being naughty, a smile from their faces would stop me from being mad. But of course it would not deter me to explain to them the consequences of their actions. Every time we came home from a hard day's work at the office, a smile from the faces of our loved ones would always bring sunshine, joy and relief.

A smile can be infectious. If you are surrounded by people who are happy and smile, you feel comfortable and at ease, and at times you can alleviate your problems. Smiling can also have a tremendous effect on your health by lowering your stress level, hence leaving less negativity and a more positive outlook on life.

This is one of the best quotes from Mother Theresa, a recently canonised saint: "Every time you smile at someone, it is an action of love, a gift to that person, a beautiful thing." An awe inspiring and impressive quote that is always worth remembering.

You can do no wrong by smiling. It is good for the body and smiling symbolises contentment, peace and positive attitude. There is so much anger, negativity and chaos at present, and what the world needs now is smiling and happy people regardless of what the situation is. So keep on smiling and as the popular saying goes: "Smile and the world smiles at you, cry and you will cry alone."

Some of my original and unpublished quotes about smiles:

A smile can do wonder
It denotes friendship,
Peace and love

A beautiful smile coming from your loved one
Always brings inspiration and love
Especially when you are at the lowest ebb of your life

Just a simple smile
A warm hello
And a gracious thank you
Would make anyone's day

10
The Realities of Life

Just a simple, gentle squeeze on your hand from someone you love, can mean a thousand things. A wonderful token of love, affection, care, understanding, support and much more. It can be easily felt within your heart, a simple gesture, yet stronger and powerful, than any spoken words.

I do believe, it's not only saying "I love you," but it's all about caring and even doing sacrifices if needed for someone you love.

Love for me is the essence of what life is all about, happy are those who are surrounded with loved ones; faithful friends, and most of all loving families. These are the very people who will always be there for you regardless of what you are.

Of course it is not always easy for us to make choices, at times we falter along the way. People will despise, criticise, but you can still manage to be strong. You know there are those who believe in you. They are the reason for your inspiration to fight back until you can achieve your dreams and goals in life.

However there are those who are consumed by success, forgetting where they started. When everything had been taken away from them, they realised who their real friends are. They sought out the loving arms of their families.

We don't have to please everyone, there are people who won't appreciate you no matter what you do. Instead, concentrate more on those who love and care for you. They will always be there for you, thus making your journey easier and more meaningful.

You can read more of my inspirational messages from my two books. *My Innermost Thoughts* is a compilation of my poems, wisdoms, and beliefs. *My Passion My Calling* is a memoir, encompassing my journey as an author.

An excerpt from *My Innermost Thoughts*: "Why would I want all the wealth in the world? Why would I want all the fame and glory, where I don't know who are my real friends and enemies? Yes it's true, there are those who have both fame and glory, yet they don't have the peace within themselves. Out of desperation, their only way is to drown in drugs and alcohol, and then find themselves more confused, that will lead them to self-destruction and even death. I don't envy them. I think as long as I have enough to live, surrounded with people I love and trust. *I feel I am the luckiest person on earth*

17
The Art of Friendship

LOVE comes in many different forms, and one of them is in the form of *friendship*. A friend can be a mother, sister, or husband, but what I will be discussing in this article is the strong attraction within the interpersonal relationship between two people.

Since time immemorial, all of us have sought and pursued someone to trust, hence friendships blossom. Some friendships continue to exist from childhood up to the present that last forever; truly the best friendships to be desired.

There are times that we can only confide our darkest and innermost secret thoughts to our best friends, and not to our parents or loved ones. This is a token of reliance and loyalty that you are confident to share to your best friend. Friendship is unconditional, forgiving, and has a mutual understanding of each other. However, I strongly believe that in order for friendship to flourish and survive both should take responsibility to nurture it. To make an effort to negotiate what is fair for the interest of both sides.

Oftentimes we develop friendship with a person whom we share the same interests and beliefs. Different personalities can clash, but in rare cases friendships can also develop for two people who have different backgrounds and cultures. Likewise it can also be built based off compatibility either emotionally, spiritually, and psychologically.

A true friend will be able to tell you the truth - even if it hurts – with the intention to do what is best for you. A friend will always be there for you, especially during vulnerable moments in your life. Indeed it is a beautiful expression of friendship.

There are different levels of friendship, the first being your very best friend, and second, casual friends – the friends you associate with time to time and still consider to be a good friend. The third is a group of social friends who are bound together with the same objectives or goals, for example the friends that you have in different organisations doing the same activities or hobbies. The fourth kind are the internet friends such as Facebook friends, a sign of the modern technology of today.

Oftentimes I met with a group of friends who I have lunch with on a weekly basis. When we catch up with each other we share stories of whatever interests us. These are the friends that I have known for the decades since I came to Australia. With them is a day of laughter and jubilation.

One of the best examples of the true definition of what friendship is portrayed in the movie *Beaches*. Presumably most of us have seen this captivating story about two friends. Though they did have differences, her friend stood beside her and helped her go through her difficult times.

So what makes a best friend so special? Is it because you have the privilege of choosing a friend? Or is it because you know that your friend will always be there for you regardless. Whatever the reasons are, one thing is certain: friends will make us feel comfortable and important. They can bring out the best in us, and for me that is what friendships are all about.

Friendship

True friendship does not take
A day to make
It takes fine wine years to age
And to attain perfection
Friendship takes years to develop
Those memories good ones and bad ones
You share together
Accepting of ones faults

And indifferences
Understanding and forgiveness
And if time comes when you don't see each other again
Beautiful memories of friendship
That no one can take away from you
Will remain embedded in your heart

18
Chrysalis My Journey as an Author

(Excerpt from my book My Passion My Calling)

Every Sunday morning as often as possible, we attended mass in our community Parish church. Today's Sunday was no different. It was bright sunny day, Chris and I decided to take a walk after mass in the nearby Tea Garden Park opposite our house. We hurriedly went home and changed to our walking gear.

I do love walking with Chris, admiring those majestic trees along the river banks of the Maribyrnong river. And also feasting my eyes with the natural rock formations of different shapes and colours.

The Tea Garden is complete with barbecue facilities and I playground ideal for families get together. Remember Chris? When our children were young they loved this place. Yes I know how time flies now it is just the two of us. Chris said with a sadness in his voice. Be happy Chris you have two beautiful grandchildren and you still have me, I replied.

Feeling tired after walking for few hours I said " Chris I am tired I've had enough. Let's start walking home. Chris agreed " okay we will head home and rest

It was almost noon so I prepared our lunch then rested and

watched TV. Suddenly I felt an intense pain at the back of my abdomen spreading to my groin and leg. I am with pain and scream; Chris help I need help ! Chris rushed from the bedroom into the family room. Evelyn what's wrong honey I will call triple 000

My face was pale then I felt blood coming from my behind. I was bleeding heavily. Ambulance came and drove me to Western General Hospital. I was given a blood transfusion ,subjected to a CT scan that found out I had an abdominal aneurysm. I undergone a procedure called Aneurysm Embolisation, a risky procedure that can damaged the bowel and surrounding vessels.

After more than three hours of surgery I felt coldness beginning at my feet, envelop my whole body. It seemed as though the world stood still and that I had travelled through time. Serenity, complete peace, calmness. …I experienced all of these. Then I saw rows of flowers, their fragrances greeting my senses. My whole body was feeling light as if I was walking in clouds. My surroundings were all in white.

At the far end I could visualise a tunnel and at the end of the tunnel a striking glittering brightness that almost blinded my eyes. I would have liked to have gone inside but my mind was saying no. Slowly I walked to the tunnel but at the moment I tried to step inside the door shut.

Then I woke up and heard the nurse saying " Mrs Valdez stay with us open your eyes. She kept doing a tender slap on my face. She said urgently " Doc, the blood pressure is at dangerous level even the heart beat and pulse are low" The Doc said" Only a few seconds more I think I have done it well. Lets hope no complications will happen. The procedure lasted almost four hours ,I had used so many litres of blood that it seemed that my entire blood must have been replenished. Then they moved me to a recovery room. The following day the surgeon visited me in my room and said" I am happy with the outcome. According to the scan the coil was successfully placed at the ruptured blood vessel. I did not tell my family what had happened at the theatre

Months passed I was doing well, full of energy and back to my routine. It was Father's Day, all my family was at my place. I was busy cooking ,but I always treasured the special moments to be with loved ones. At this time I asked Michelle my daughter to sign me up on face book. She laughed and said" Mum you hate writing and besides Face Book is only for young ones. With my persistence she obliged. I surprised myself I could write. I didn't know where my thoughts and ideas were coming from. Each time I was at the computer I started writing poems, inspirational messages and quotes, all base on my strong beliefs and convictions. Never in my wildest dreams did I imagine I would be able to do it.

Chris could see the change in me and one day at the breakfast table he asked" Evelyn what's got in to you? You started having interest in writing, which I know you always hated I have not heard you play for decades, but now you started tickling the ivory keys.. What has happened? I Replied I do not have any explanation Chris, I just feel my passion for writing and music in my heart. He responded" I think there is something that has happened to trigger you enthusiasm. I said" I can not think of anything else except that I was hospitalised for abdominal aneurysm. Chris laughed and said 'HA HA HA you believe that, you and your imagination.

For almost one and a half years I kept on writing until one afternoon another ordeal in my life happened. Chris was beside me at our kitchen bench table while I was sorting out oye groceries, suddenly I had double vision, passed out for few seconds. I found myself in the arms of Chris, preventing me from falling and hitting my head on the floor. Ambulance was called and I was rushed to the Western General Hospital. The MRI confirmed that I had a congenital brain aneurysm. It was only small so it was inoperable. I was given a blood thinning tablet and with healthy diet ,it will be controlled.

After this frightening episode, I decided to write a book to have a legacy for my family, friends and relations. I started organising and accumulating all my writings from Facebook and my notes and scribbles. I found it daunting organising everything . It took me few weeks to accomplish it. My manuscript was sent to many publishers. Being an unknown author I found it difficult. Several publishers rejected my work. Feeling disappointed and frustrated, I turned to my husband and said " Chris I don't think I will have a chance to pursue my dream. Chris said" Don't stop following your dream . Keep on trying, I know you will be able to make it.. This is typical of Chris, my very supportive husband, who was always giving hope and encouragement about what I was doing.

Browsing through the internet, I came across a publishing company, I rang them and they agreed to have a look at my manuscript. It was a nervous wait. Two weeks passed, feeling nervous but hopeful, I received an email from the publisher. The editor loved my manuscript and recommended for publication I jumped with joy, ran to Chris who was busy at the backyard, hugged him and screamed at the top of my voice 'Chris at last I will be an author. Chris said " I am overjoyed and very happy for you Evelyn, I 've had faith always in you. I always knew you can do it.

Finally I received the first copy of the book, impressed with the book I ordered two hundred copies. The whole family was excited especially my granddaughter Kaitlin who said" Wow Grandma this is the first time my name is in the book. I said "Of course, sweetie. This will not be the last time more will be coming. Then her eyes brightened and she gave me a hug

I then organised two book launches at my place. All the family were involved in presentation and arrangement. My son -in law Edward suggested that I should have a launch in Bendigo, saying quite a few people would be interested in buying the book. The following month in the last month of August my book was launched at Bendigo .My son in-law's family and friends and all of my families were there to support me. I was excited and quite nervous but it turned out to be a success. One of the Edward's family friend invited me for a afternoon tea, Of course I said yes. My children and their partners headed home, Simone and Kaitlin stayed with us.

Edward's friend's place was beautiful, Emma and her husband George were lovely couple and very friendly. Rows of beautiful geranium, roses and begonias of different colours were planted in the front yard, mixed with native shrubs and trees. They had a big veranda at the back of the house where we have our tea, biscuits and cakes.

The children Kaitlin and Simone were playing football in the spacious backyard full of fruit trees, a veggie patch and again rows of beautiful roses and geraniums. Even the Veranda was filled with hanging begonias of different colours. Chris and George were busy tackling politics, and other topics. As I entered the veranda I felt something ---as if I knew the place. Sitting at the veranda having a cup of tea , Emma said " I wish my daughter Tessa was here. I said where is Tessa now? Tears started to fill Emma's eyes. She's gone four years ago in a car accident 16th of May 2010 at 4:00 pm

I experienced goose bumps ,cold shivers and shock I could hardly breathe — that day I will always remember. May 16, 2010 at 4:00 pm was when I had a near death experience during my abdominal surgery. Emma said " What's wrong Mrs Valdez? You feeling okay you looked pale, want a glass of water? I am okay no problem Thanks. Emma continued " Tessa loved poetry and always dreamed one day of having her book published.

She was also a good classical pianist. We really miss her. I will show you her room still untouched exactly as it was before she died. I will also show you all her writings. They are almost identical as yours. Please come inside.

I followed Emma inside. Again I had a feeling of familiarity with the place as if I had been here all my life. Her room "Tessa" was at the far end , the first room near the front door. We entered the bedroom: again the smell, the sights were so close to my senses and heart. Familiarity reigned once more.

Emma handed me a neatly kept file of writings inside an envelope. Upon reading Tessa's writings I realised that although different words were used, the meanings, themes. Messages were almost identical to mine.

I heard Chris's voice at the veranda saying "C'mon Evelyn we have to keep moving. The grandchildren have to be dropped off at their place.. I replied ' Okay Chris". I kissed and hugged Emma and George. Such a lovely couple to lose their only child. I did not say anything about the connection between Tessa and me.

Emma said "It was strange but I could feel I had a good connection with you the moment I saw you. I said "Same with me Emma. Really nice meeting both of you and for sure this will not be our last time. Hope we will be seeing each other some time. Emma replied "Of course you can visit us anytime and you can bring your grand children. They are so adorable.

Driving home that afternoon, I was quiet, Chris looked at me and said" Evelyn you have not said a word since we left. Anything bothering you? I Replied "Its okay I just feel exhausted after a long day. Nothing to worry about. But in my mind I know the reason why I was still here.......To continue the mission and calling. One day I will explain to Chris and to the beautiful couple Emma and George. That will be ....when the time is right.

There are some things in our lives
We can not comprehend or explain
Beautiful moment can always happen
Always Chase your DREAMS and your DESTINY
BY Lorna Ramirez

Inspirational Messages and Thoughts

There is nothing more stronger and admirable than the hearts
who care, share and understand

No one is too old to continue chasing their passions.
Just focus and persevere till you
Reach your goal.

Truly I can say there are friends who are worth keeping
And those you can live without
Treasure those who are!

We laughed, we cried
We loved, we grieved
Have you learned something from these?

What is the secret of a successful person?
They always remain humble
And they don't forget their root and the people
Who helped them

Expectations will always lead
To heartaches and disappointments
Its nice to be surprised

Although the passing years had taken away
Our youthful and physical beauty, but through
The years it strengthen our souls and changed
Our perspective in life

It is in what we believe
That makes us strong
It is in whom we love
That inspires us

I had done my legacy
And fully satisfied with my life
Regardless of whatever happens

With every breath I take
With every sigh I made, the thought of you
Will forever embedded in my heart

It is in the mother's love
We can realised what loving
Is all about

There are some moments
In your life worth reminiscing
And will always have
Special place in your heart

Sometimes negativity from others
Will inspire you to achieve
Your utmost goal
And proven them wrong

Life is such a big lottery
You do not have a choice
Coming here on earth

Life will be empty
Without love, dreams, and convictions

In love we can rediscover
Our inner self
And our hidden strength

There are times in your life
A certain event that happened
Will entirely change
Your perspective in life

Chasing your dream is one thing
Taking action is another story

Running away for things that matter
Will only lead to disappointments

True love will always
Find the way

Declutter your heart with unimportant things
To let "HIM" reign in your heart

Fame and success will not guarantee
The "Holy Grail" of happiness
And peace within

Whenever you are at your lowest ebb
Just think of all your blessings
Your smile will be back

Life is not always a bed of roses
Learn to deal with good and bad ones
Many things we can encounter
As we walk the journey of our lives

It is not the quantity
But the quality of friends
That matter most

Be not deceived by smiling faces
At times their hearts
Are as cold as Ice

If you are constantly blaming others
And not accepting responsibilities for your actions
You will never find the reason
For your existence here on earth

Sometimes choosing which passion to follow
Is akin to choosing who is your favourite child

It really feels good if you do not expect
Anything and if the outcome is surreal
Happiness

Realities of life…At times
New friends are the ones who
Will support you and your advocacy

To have a strong belief will
Inspire a person to follow
Their passions. Dreams and goals in life

It is so easy for us to see the faults of others
But blinded to see our own inadequacies
Its easy for us to judge others

But we react negatively, when being judge
It's easy for us to point the mistake of others
But defensive when it is our mistakes
Though no one is perfect
Being aware of all your shortcomings
Is vital for improvement, hence you can be
A better person than you are now

Start with a dream
Then the imaginary concept
Becomes a Reality
The result will be an ultimate HAPPINESS

I believe a person is considered Rich
Not by material wealth
And not by what he has
But by what he is

Regardless of whatever be the situations
Always be yourself
And it will work out for the best

Traumatizing moments are only temporary
What matters most
Are lessons learned from these

Material things will come and go
But the purity, honest and kindness

Of your spiritual soul
Will always be remembered

Transform your heartaches, failures and disappointments
Into one whole -learning experience and wisdom
For one's self and others

Do not crucify yourself by doing things
Just because people are expecting you to do
Do the things you enjoy and love doing
This way you are making the favour for yourself

There are those who lived their whole lives
Without finding love
Lucky are those even though
Their lives are cut short
They had experienced
How it is to love and be loved.

Your priority in life
And what matters to you
Will truly define
Who you are

Without sorrow and pain
We won't know the real meaning of happiness
Without love there is no joy of living
Without faith and hope

We won't have any strength and inspiration
Most importantly
Without our strong connection with GOD
We will find it hard to go
Through the hard times and trial in our lives

True love lingers on
Up to the last breath of our lives
Sacrifices will turn to glory
For the one you love and adore

The magical power of a camera
Capturing that beautiful second
Of motion and moment, that only
A click of the camera can do
This can not be retrieved nor repeated

The realization of my dream
Is my Holy Grail

If your heart is filled with love
And care, giving and sharing
Will always be easy

Pretence and hypocrisy will never last
At the end you can no longer
Hide behind the mask
Truth will prevail

There are things that we cannot bring back
What had been taken from us
Enjoy what was left
To bring closure
To our lives

In times of sorrow
We prayed and remember Him
In times of abundance
Do we still remember Him?

Rejection, disappointments are sometimes
Can make you stronger
More determined than ever
To do things you are passionate about
These are the catalysts that can
Drive you to success, to seek perfection
Until you can achieve all the goals
You are aiming for

We try so hard deceiving others
But at the end we get confused
Who we really are

It is in what we believe
That will shape
Our Present and future life

A life full of love
Is life full of bliss

The most beautiful things in life
That can not be touch nor seen
Is called LOVE

All of us have gone through several stages in life
Each stage is a learning experience
At the end it is nice to look back
Not counting the years you have gone through
But counting the special moments
That you had been through

It does not matter what they say
It does not matter what they think of you
It does not matter how they judge you
What matters most is being happy
Happy for the things you do
And believing in yourself

The past will have a big impact
Of what we are now
Others will move on
But there are those who will be ruined
And scarred for life

Life is so simple
Why do we have to make it so complicated?
Aftermath of modern civilization

It is who I am that matters
And not what you want me to be

It is not about making it to the top
Being successful and famous in your career
It is all about giving back
Generously to the community
Some of your time
Specially to those needing the most

Letting it go does not mean forgetting the past
It is merely a preparation
For the new beginning
New life, new hope
Use your past as an inspiration
For a better future

Amidst your frustrations and disappointments
These will help you re-evaluate
Your priorities in life
What is important and what is not

Do not underestimate the power of words
The power of writing
It can do more harm than you ever realise
It can destroy a person's reputation

We should always know our own limitations
The time to stop and re-assess your priority
At times we are so immersed in our fame and success
That we think we are indestructible
Soon it is too late to know that we are not

Words are more lethal and fatal weapon
At times it go straight to your heart
And the pain is so excruciating

It is your choice, your decision
To make your life fruitful or a failure
Happiest moments in my life
Is when surrounded by my loved ones

THE PURSUIT OF HAPPINESS

Waking up each day without
Expecting anything
Always thanking each day
For my blessings I have
Savouring each moment
What life has to offer
Enjoying the fullest
The beautiful surroundings
Beautiful people such as
Loved ones and friends
Whom they had given me joy
And making my journey of life
Interesting and meaningful
And most importantly
Had a part of making me
What I am today

At times we falter and failed
But that is not important
What matters most
Is how quickly we stand up
And do it all over again
This time we had learned your lesson
And we are more prepared than ever
And more determined to succeed
The second time around

Others hide their sorrows through their smiles
Others hide their fears by acting fearlessly
Others hide their insecurity by being boastful all the time
Others hide their inferiority by
acting superior to everyone
At times things that we see are not really what they are
There are more depths and meanings to consider
BEFORE JUDGING

MY FAITH
With every quest I had gone through
With every trial I had endured
With every frustration I had suffered
With every fall I had
Without a doubt in my mind
I will be able to overcome all these
Because I know these trying times
God will guide and lead me
To find the right path to cross

Trust should be balanced
Too trusting
You will find yourself
Taken advantage
While not trusting anyone
At times can be a miss opportunity

True character of a person
Will be revealed
If intoxicated frustrated and angry

Love is always forgiving, understanding and caring

Just like respect, trust
Should be earned
And not be given freely

Have you ever wonder and be bewildered
By the beauty and fragrance of the rose?
Amidst the thorns, that can symbolise our sufferings
Our trials and tribulations
Once conquered at the end is
The beautiful glorious beauty of a Rose
That symbolise our achievement

It is in what we believe
That will shape our present
And future life

I wish I could be remembered
Not by who I was
But what I was
And the things I did
During my living years

At times we can learn
Something
From the innocence, purity
And unadulterated mind
Of a child

There are moments that the
Sweetest words to be heard
Are those that are yet unspoken
And still buried in one's heart

It is not the quantity of friends
But the quality of friends matter

The safest place to be
Is in someone's heart and mind
Who will always love and care for you
And will always be there for you
Regardless

Everything done in excess
Becomes a poison
Irrespective of what they are

The worst regret in my life
Is not doing enough
What my heart desires
Not knowing of the possible results

A person who always lies
At the end will not know
The difference
Between the truth and the lies

Our conscience is responsible
For making us of what we are today
It helps shapes our beliefs, convictions
And our character. However there are times
It can be overtaken by greed such as power, fame and money
Let us hope we can be aware
Of these temptations

Life is full of surprises and regardless
Of what they are we should always
Be prepared and flexible
And be able to cope everything
That cross our path
Lucky are those who have support
From families and friends
But think of those
Who got no one to turn to

We do not expect to live forever
So make each day a celebration of life
Each day thanking him for
All the graces we have
Savour each precious moment
You spend with loved ones, families and friends
If you fail to do so
You will miss the most important
Things in your life
That money could not buy

It is in the realm of one's experience
That we learn to know
What is right or wrong
What is ethical or not
But some are just too stubborn
To accept their past mistakes
Relentlessly doing the same mistakes
Over and over again

There are moments
That are precious
That we tend to relive and remember
Each time. It makes us happy and puts
A smile on our faces
But there are memories that should be
Forgotten and instead serve as a lesson
Learned in our lives

Sometimes what we had seen and perceived
Are not really what they are. Because often times
Evil can mask in the shadow of goodness

An act of kindness
Done whole heartedly
One should not expect
Anything in return

In the midst of darkness
Love will always find its way
And brightens your path

There are those people who
Are getting their satisfaction by acting aggressively
To free themselves from the wrong deeds they had done
A subtle way of self-gratification

Such a beautiful gesture of friendship
When they are always there
To help you in time of needs
Support you in time of sorrow
Guide and lead you
When you are confused, and lost
For sure they are worth more than gold

Victory will be joyful and glorious
After each peril we had gone through

Without your faith and guidance
From God, you will be lost
Like a child wandering in the forest
With nowhere to go
And through "Him" you will see
The light and the way

Do not just follow the flow
Scrutinise, analyse
And it will lead you
To the right path

Greed, megalomaniac
Are akin to cancer
Slowly creeping and destroying
Your soul

One should always be wary
If you are only being used
For their own personal interest

A kind- hearted person
Will always see the goodness
Of others

Hurting and demeaning a person
Is not an option
And should always be avoided

The worst part of human behaviour
Is stepping someone's toes
Just to achieve their goals

We are so conscious
About the issue of political correctness
That refrain us from voicing our opinion

Loving someone has its negative side
You feel the pain when you see them hurting
You worry and pray that nothing will happen to them
You wish and hope that they will be able to cope up
With the challenges along the way
In spite of these I will say
These are only a small price to pay
For the blessings, blissful happiness
And joy of having someone to love
And in return to be loved.

Precious friends will become
Strangers due to unforeseen circumstance

I am meek as a lamb
But once Threaten and taken advantage of
I will be as ferocious as a lion

Greed, hungry for power, divide a nation
Destroyed friendship
Split families…… Harsh realities of life

Doesn't matter how and what they think of you
What matters is following your conscience
Following the truth

I believe that the main question about life
Is not all about yourself
But its all about what you had done
To help others, love others as you love yourself
To use your talents not only for yourself
But also for the benefit of mankind

Anything fighting
For a cause
Is worthwhile
Regardless of the aftermath

In times of trouble
You will know and realised
Who are your genuine friends

Amidst the turmoil and pain
Have faith in "Thee"
Solutions will be on your way

We tried as much as we can to hold on something
No matter how precious it was
There will come a time
We have to let it go
And continue to move on

You won't be able to see
What lies beneath
The mountain
Till you have the courage to climb it

Evil is around and within us
If you let it conquer you
It will destroy your body, spirit and soul

Happy are those who can forgive
Because they can easily attain
Inner peace within themselves
And fellowman

Reliving the moments
Of once beautiful memories
Can always bring
Sunshine and hope
Especially when one
Is in the middle
Of a personal conflict

Though we are human
We still have the power to choose
To be evil and righteous
To be a success or a failure
To be miserable and happy
To be moral and indecent
To be just or unjust
To be truthful or deceitful
Whatever you choose
Will determine
Who and what you will be
Now and the future
You should be responsible for your life
And no one else

Perhaps the most agonising
Pain of all
Is the one still deep in your heart
That no one can see or tell
But you are the only one
Who can feel and bear

Don't let your generosity
Be against you
At times people can
Manipulate and abuse you
For their own benefit

And satisfaction

Mother

When no one can understand me

My mother will

When no one loves me

My mother will

With all her heart

When I am all alone and in sorrow

My mother will

Comfort me

When I am confused and no where to go

My mother will

Guide and lead me

No one can have such a kind of love

Such a deep and intense love of a mother

It is up for us to live our life

To the fullest

Age is not a barrier

To do things

You are passionate about

There will always be a room

For improvement

Discovering your self

And never stop

Your quest for knowledge

TO ALL MOTHERS

Each gift of the breath of life
A mother plays a crucial part
Suffice to say
It is indeed deserving
To celebrate the most important
Person on earth
MOTHERS
They are so forgiving, and understanding
They will always be there for you
Regardless of all circumstances
Knows the real essence
Of what sacrifices is all about
A wonderful loved person by all

GIFT TO MANKIND
EXCERPT FROM MY BOOK
My Innermost Thoughts
It is with giving that we find the joy of sharing
It is in loving that we can fully feel how it is to be loved
It is in understanding that we can practise the art of compassion
It is in believing in ourselves that we can focus and do
Anything our heart desire
And most importantly
It is in trusting and believing in him
That we can find all the inspiration and courage to do these things

Giving does not mean expecting
To receive in return
Loving does not mean
Changing the person
For your own self intent
Believing does not mean
Being blinded and shielded
From facing the truth
Hoping does not mean
Not realising
Your own limitations and inadequacies

Always be wary because at times
You will see is only an illusion
And can be deceiving

To invest in education
Is the most noble charity
You can give to all
Especially those needing the most

At times to be hurt is needed"
To evaluate your past
Present and your future

The difference between a successful person
And a loser
The first will see opportunity around them
While the later will see negativity and often will give up
Even before trying

EXCERPT FROM MY BOOK
REFLECTIVE CONTEMPLATIONS

SIMPLE LESSONS IN LIFE

It is always best to have moments of evaluation
Assessment and recollection of the
Things happening in your life
You should make priorities of what is important
Be with people who care, love and support you
Who will be there for you
Regardless of the situation
Disconnect to those
Who don't appreciate you
Do not be affected with criticism
Instead us the criticism for your own advantage
Hence making you a better and stronger person

Any "life changing experience"
Will always make us re-assess
And evaluate our lives
There are times what was important before
Will be no longer relevant at present
You tend more to focus to the important
Things in life such as your families and friends
And less of the material things

Some people will criticise you
For what they don't have
And abhor you for your success
An ugly side of human nature

Loving and living the life you live is one thing
But loving and living your life with dignity
Honour, and stay connected with "HIM"
Are things we should aspire
And that is what matter most

Count your blessings first
Before complaining
All your miseries and frustrations
The first one will help you realise
How lucky you are than others

You cannot put a good person down
No matter how much you tried
They will survive and excel at the end

There are memories
That are too precious to be forgotten
Especially our childhood memories
They will always bring a smile to our face
Moments deeply treasured in our hearts

Everything changes
People, places, things surrounding us
We also change through the years
Physically, emotionally, and spiritually
Loving someone means continually
Accepting them for what they are today
Rather than they were yesterday

It is in what we believe and our convictions
That make us who and what we are today
It is what we fight for that
Makes us stronger than ever
And most of all
It is our love and compassion
That can easily open our hearts
So we can help the people who need the most

Those who suffered abuse
Had pain and disappointments in life
Will emerge either as
Stronger souls
Or a person full of hatred of vengeance
At the end
Becoming the abusers
Aggressors themselves

There are times
We want to leave
Away from the past
But the past never leaves us
Keeps on haunting us
Wherever and whenever we are
And it is up to us to accept
And deal with it courageously

Regardless of what had happened
Regardless of what reasons they are
One must face life with courage
Continue to move on
Just for the sake of all the people
Who still love and care for you

Always be happy and do not worry
Too much of what others will say
Follow your heart
Avoid negativity
Think positive
And you will get
Positive result

Good services to humanity
Will follow, after you forget
All your worldly desire of fame
Greed and fortune

Recipe for success
Be yourself
Stay simple
Be humble
No one wants a person
Too big for their shoes

As long as you are aware and believe
That you are in the right path
That you are making the right decision
Following what your hear dictates
Don't listen to what others will say
Be strong and firm, follow your instinct
And success is within your reach

Make each day a celebration
Of life
A life full of hope
A life full of positive attitude
Negativity will always
Produce stress and unhealthy
For the mind spirit and soul

Love is a universal language
Love encompasses everything
Defies reasons, logic and conquers
All along its path
No one can be immune to
Its power regardless of who you are

Excerpts from my book
My innermost Thoughts
Each time we breathe to live
Each time we should remember that life is a gamble
Each time is a journey because no one knows
What the future brings and holds
Yes we can try to plan and control our lives
But much to our dismay, we soon discover we can only do it
To a certain degree
If you can change things, do them better next time
Indeed , these are the realities of life

ALSO BY
LORNA RAMIREZ

Lorna Ramirez wrote this book so she could share her wisdoms with others. She has been an observer of human behaviour and emotions and has built up her own personal philosophies throughout her life. This book is a collection of her strong beliefs and convictions and offers encouragement and enlightenment to others who may be lost and confused or be looking for some positive advice and assistance. Lorna Ramirez is a woman of strong beliefs in her faith and advocates believing in oneself, perseverance when times are difficult and living in the present.

This authentic story about a Filipino migrant family settling in Melbourne in 1977 is a fascinating read, as it tells of the emotions, the ups and downs, the government assistance in those days, the practicalities, the difficulties, the sudden change of lifestyle and culture but also the joys of living in Australia in the 1970s, a 'paradise' in so many ways, with great opportunities for a good life.

The wife suddenly is confronted with severe trauma, closely followed by another, a time in their lives when everything appeared perfect. Her near death experience results in new beliefs and understanding and inspires her to write.

After a traumatic experience at the hands of four men, Eliza Martinez leaves her family and home in the Philippines to find happiness in Australia. But tragedy happens again in her life. Again she must overcome all predicaments in order to pull through and move on.

As a twist of fate makes her a victim of love, she realises the importance of having support during her journey through life. She comes to rely on her friends and family — even as she considers what it would mean to start a family of her own.

This is a story of romance, forbidden love and courage; a story of human sufferings, vulnerability and how the choices we make change our lives.

This book was written by Lorna Ramirez to reach those people who need encouragement, enlightenment and strength when facing adversities and predicaments in life. The author is a keen observer of human behaviour and emotions, and wants to share with readers young and old from all walks of life her thoughts about life in general, to encourage self-motivation, positive attitude, and believing in yourself.

With all Lorna's books and written articles in Melbourne, she has always spread and promoted the advocacy of Love, Acceptance, and Tolerance regardless of creed, race, gender and beliefs.

www.ingramcontent.com/pod-product-compliance
Lightning Source LLC
Chambersburg PA
CBHW062102290426
44110CB00022B/2680